EASY PIANO

2nd Edition

EASY CLASSICS

ISBN-13: 978-1-4234-2278-5

HAL•LEONARD®
CORPORATION

7777 W. BLUEMOUND RD. P.O. BOX 13819 MILWAUKEE, WI 53213

Visit Hal Leonard Online at
www.halleonard.com

ARIOSO
from CANTATA NO. 156

By JOHANN SEBASTIAN BACH
1685-1750

Slowly

With pedal

FÜR ELISE
(For Elisa)

By LUDWIG VAN BEETHOVEN
1770-1827

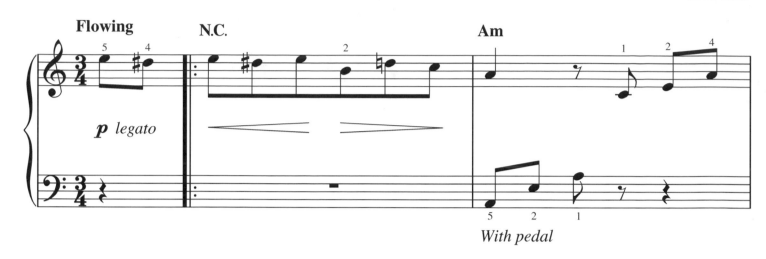

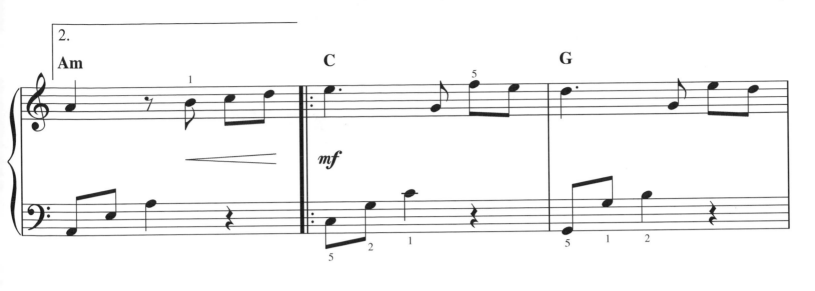

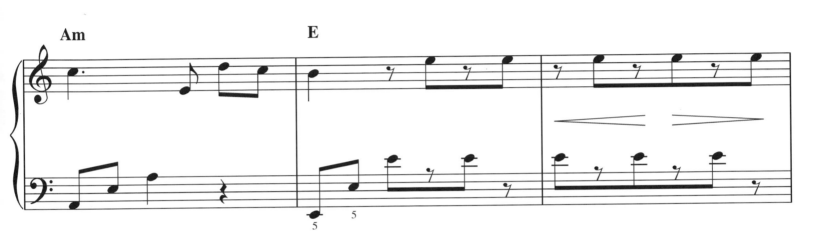

ODE TO JOY
from SYMPHONY NO. 9

By LUDWIG VAN BEETHOVEN
1770-1827

Majestically

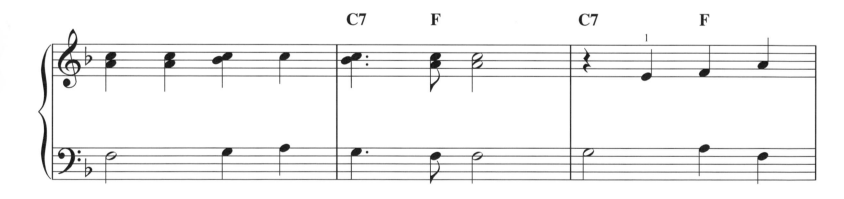

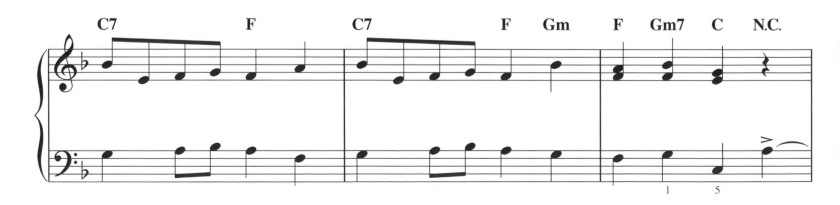

LULLABY
(Wiegenlied)

German words from *Des Knaben Wunderhorn*
Music by JOHANNES BRAHMS
1833-1897

Tenderly

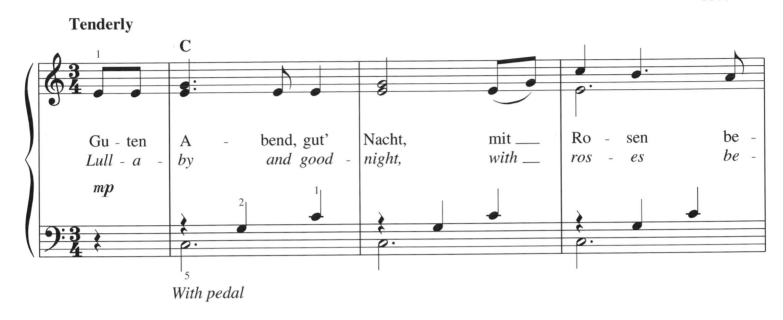

Gu - ten A - bend, gut' Nacht, mit ___ Ro - sen be -
Lull - a - by and good - night, with ___ ros - es be -

mp

With pedal

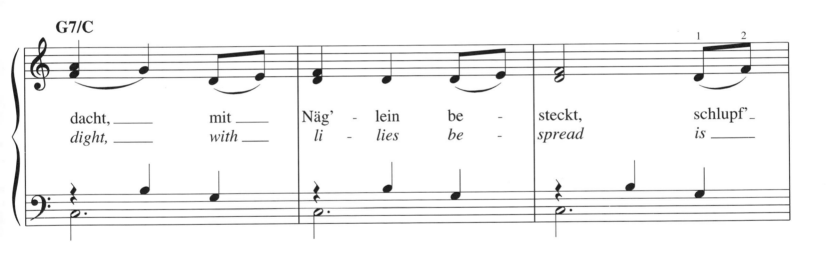

dacht, ___ mit ___ Näg' - lein be - steckt, schlupf'
dight, ___ with ___ li - lies be - spread is ___

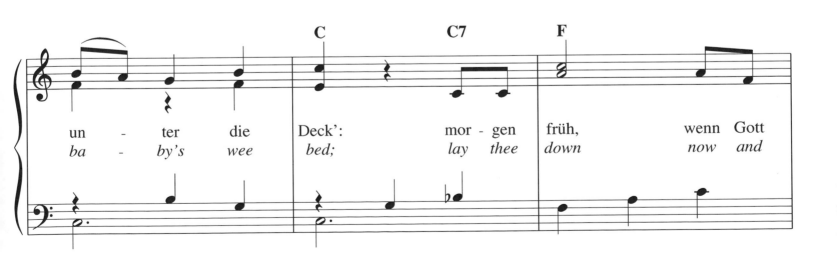

un - ter die Deck': mor - gen früh, wenn Gott
ba - by's wee bed; lay thee down now and

14

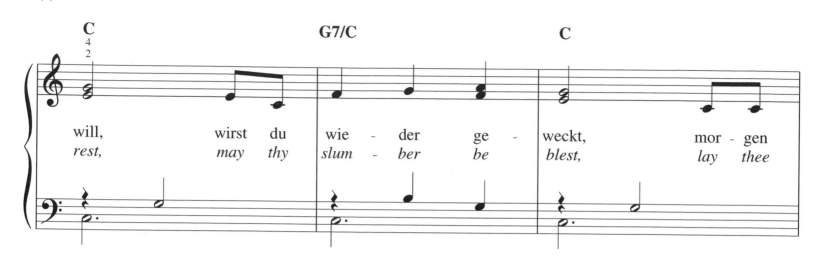

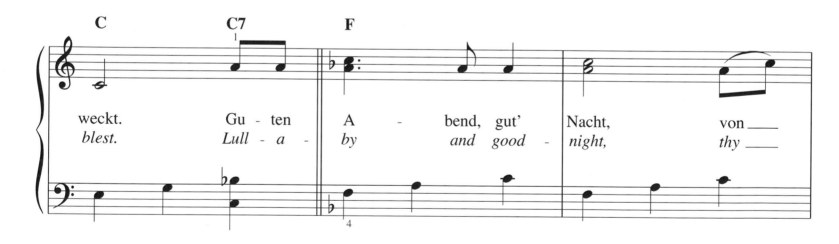

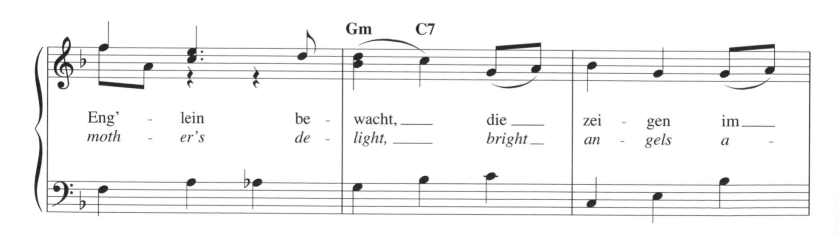

HABANERA
from CARMEN

By GEORGES BIZET
1838-1875

Allegretto quasi Andantino, in 2

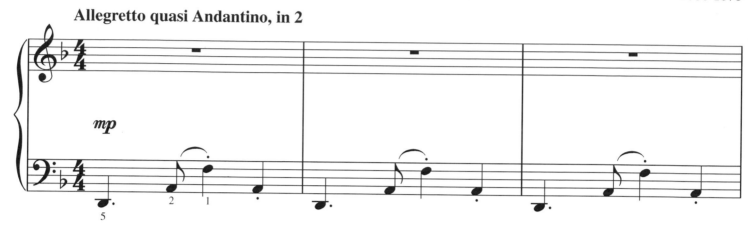

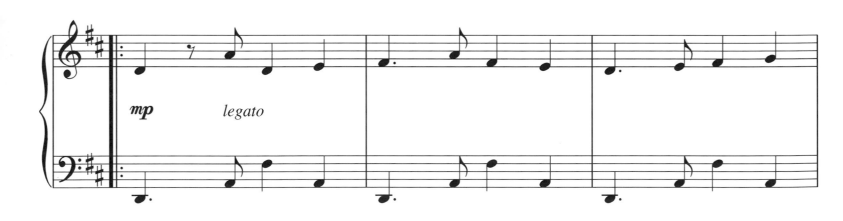

SICILIENNE

By GABRIEL FAURÉ
1845-1924

Andantino

p legato

With pedal

HALLELUJAH!

from MESSIAH

By GEORGE FRIDERIC HANDEL
1685-1759

Majestically

With pedal

24

MORNING
from PEER GYNT

By EDVARD GRIEG
1843-1907

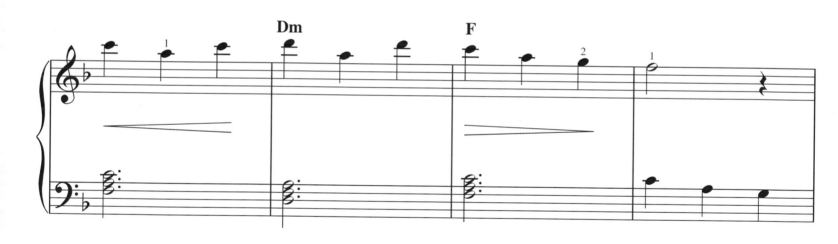

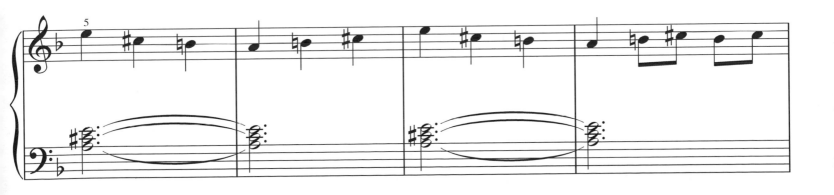

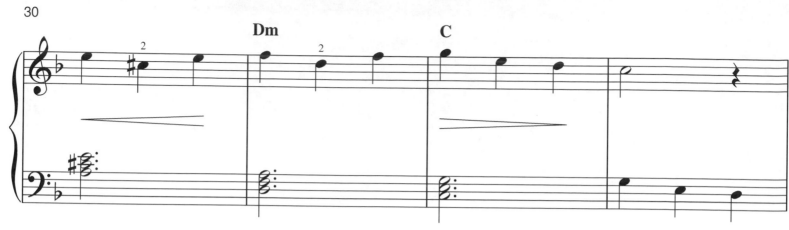

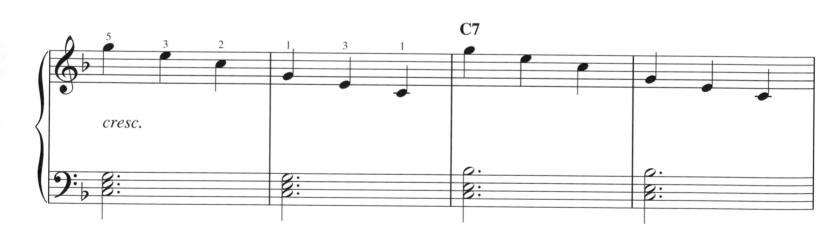

ANDANTE
from THE "SURPRISE" SYMPHONY

By FRANZ JOSEPH HAYDN
1732-1809

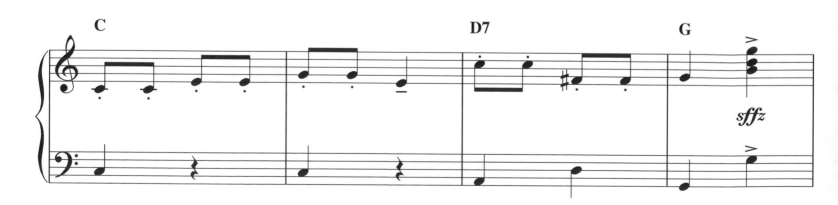

LIEBESTRAUM
(Dream of Love)

By FRANZ LISZT
1811-1886

Poco allegro

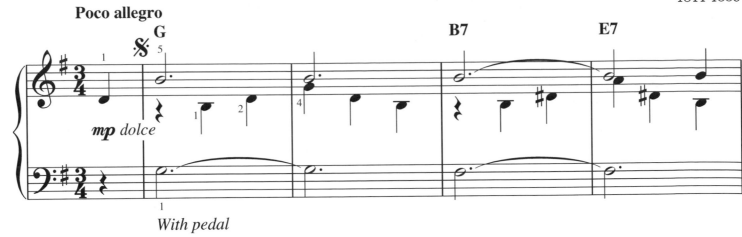

With pedal

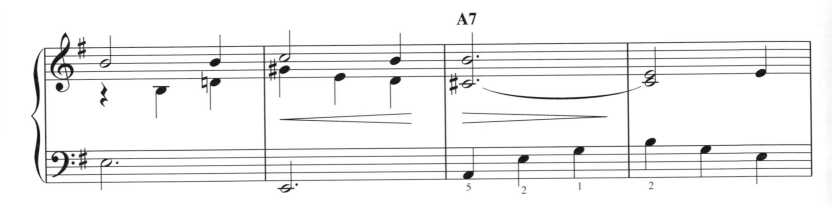

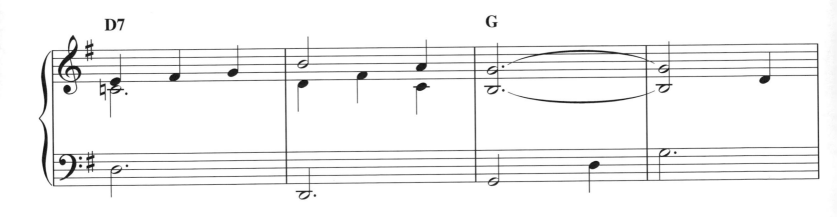

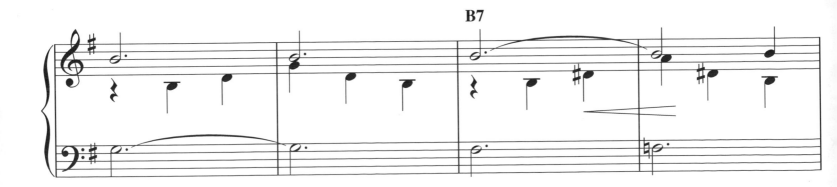

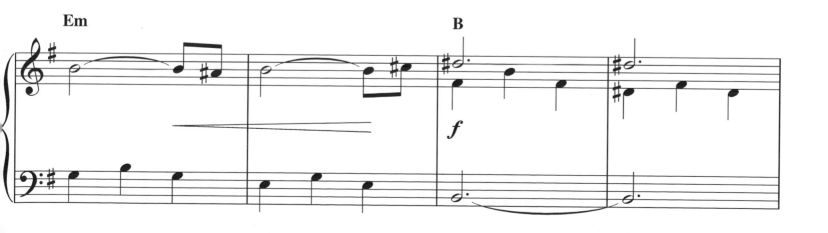

MEDITATION
from THAÏS

By JULES MASSENET
1842-1912

Moderately slow

With pedal

To Coda ⊕

A little faster

Calmly

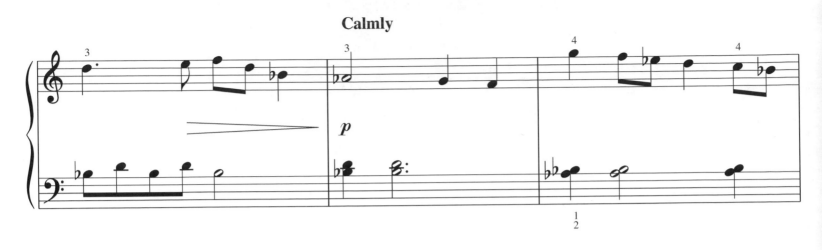

D.C. al Coda

dim. e rit.

CODA

EINE KLEINE NACHTMUSIK
First Movement Excerpt

By WOLFGANG AMADEUS MOZART
1756-1791

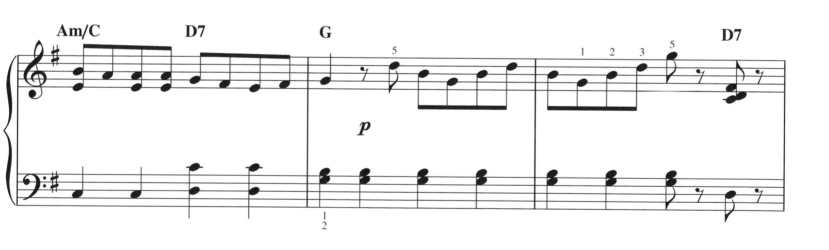

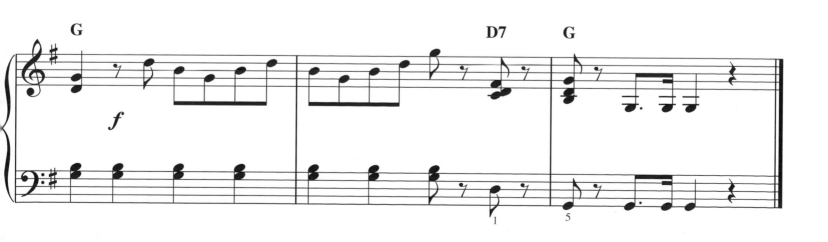

CAN CAN
from ORPHEUS IN THE UNDERWORLD

By JACQUES OFFENBACH
1819-1880

AVE MARIA

Traditional Latin text
Music by FRANZ SCHUBERT
1797-1828

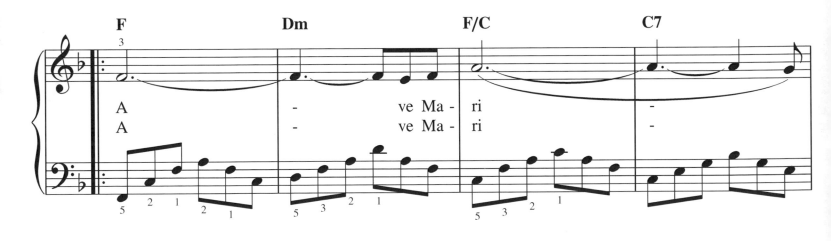

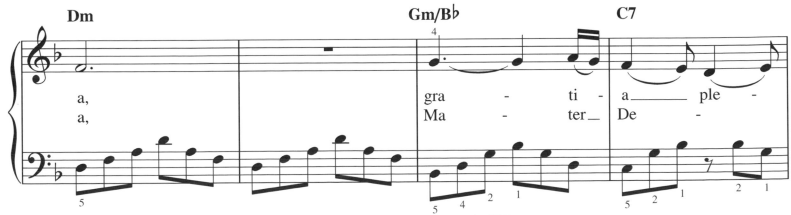

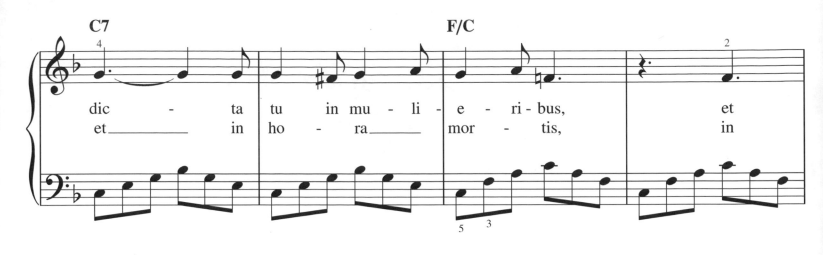

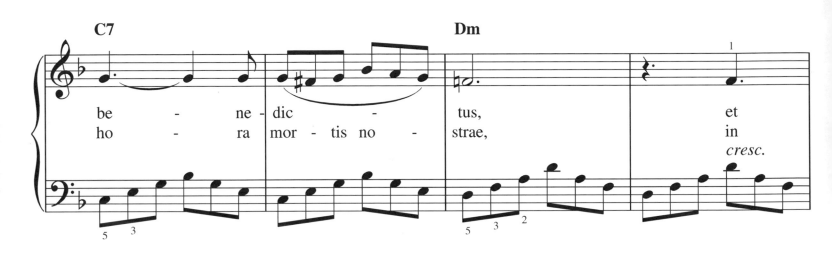

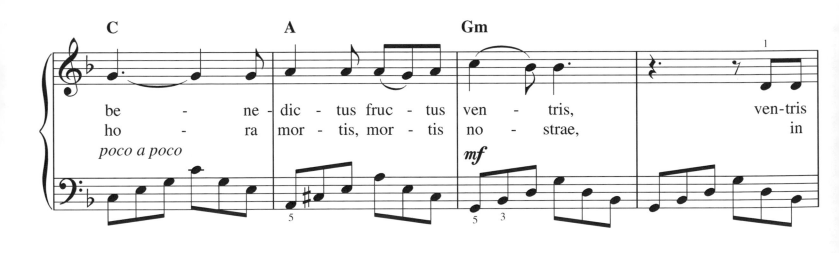

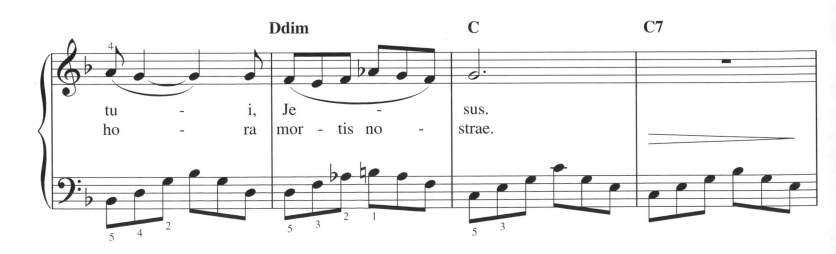

49

CANON IN D MAJOR

By JOHANN PACHELBEL
1653-1706

Slowly

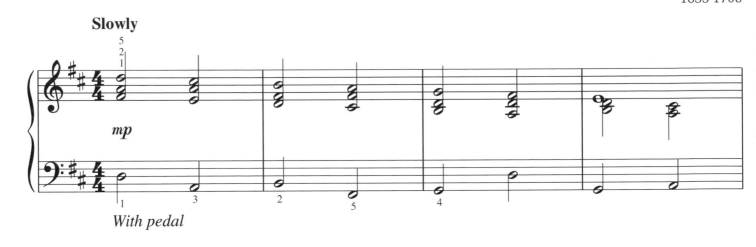

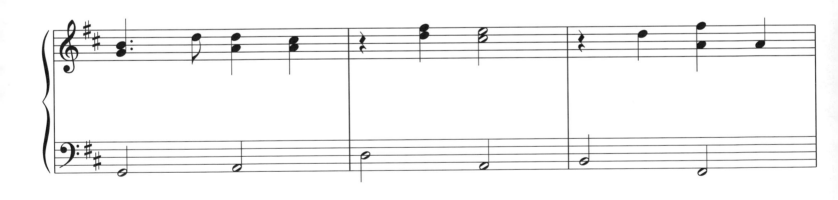

53

ROMEO AND JULIET
(Love Theme)

By PYOTR IL'YICH TCHAIKOVSKY
1840-1893

Andante, con espressione

p legato e dolce

With pedal

cresc.

mp

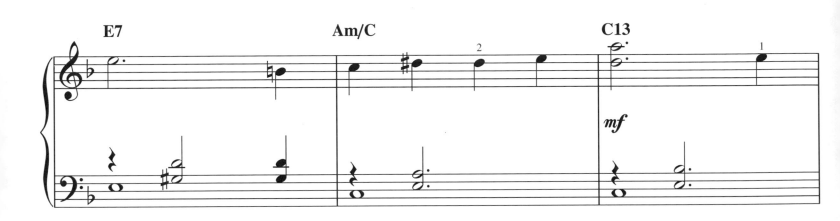

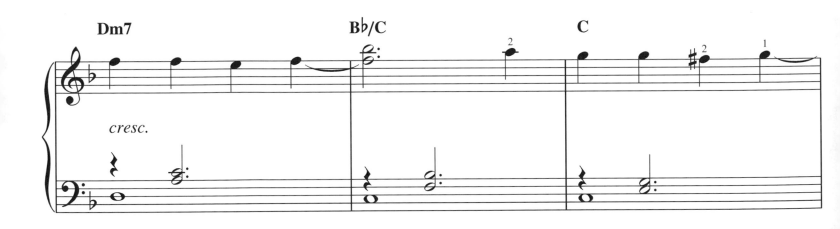

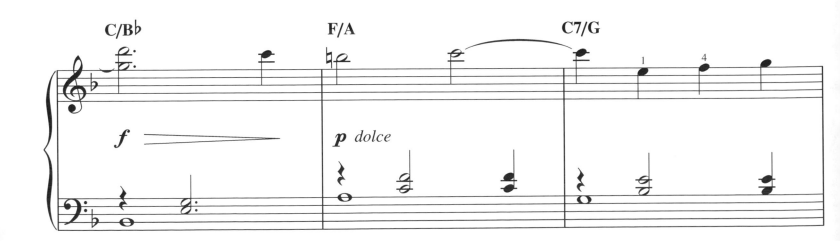

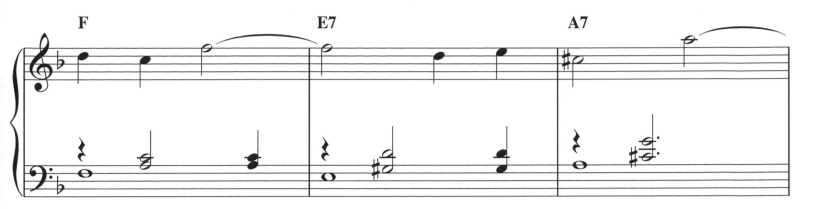

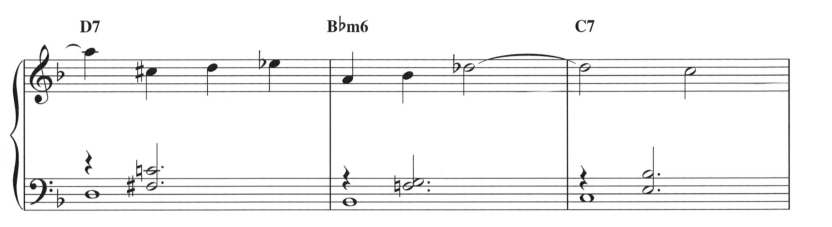

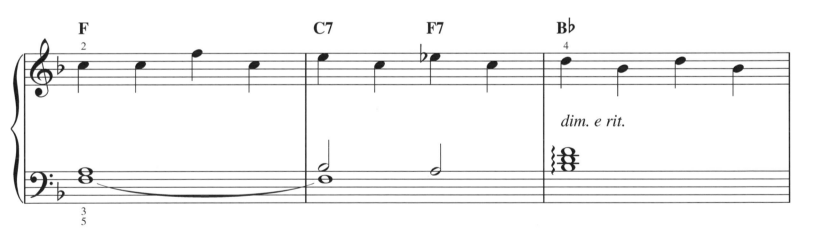

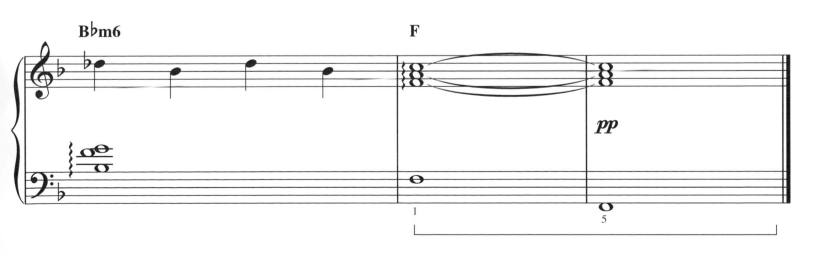

SWAN LAKE
(Principal Theme)

By PYOTR IL'YICH TCHAIKOVSKY
1840-1893

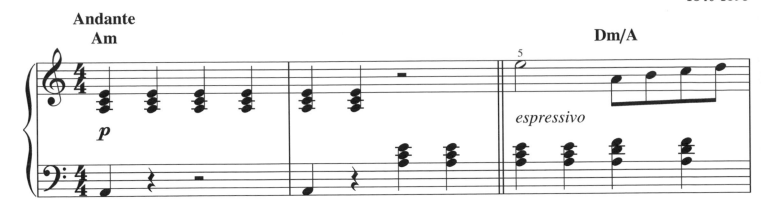

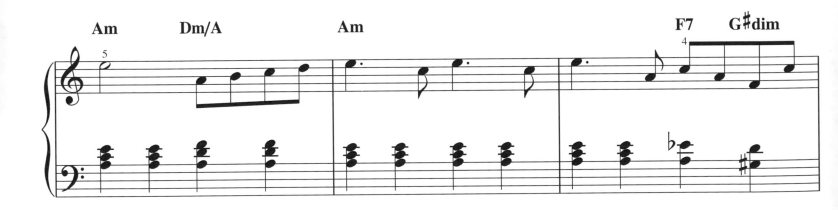

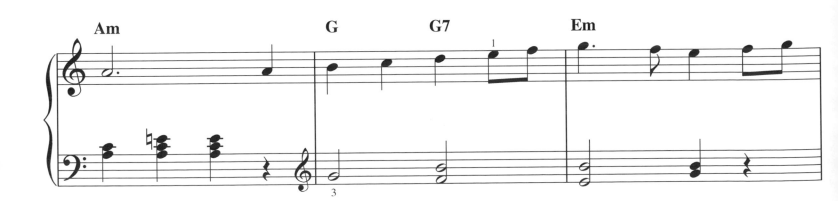

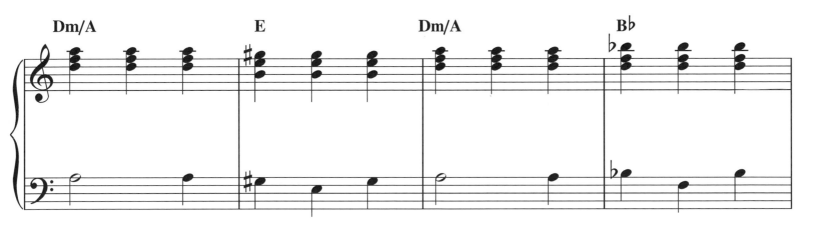

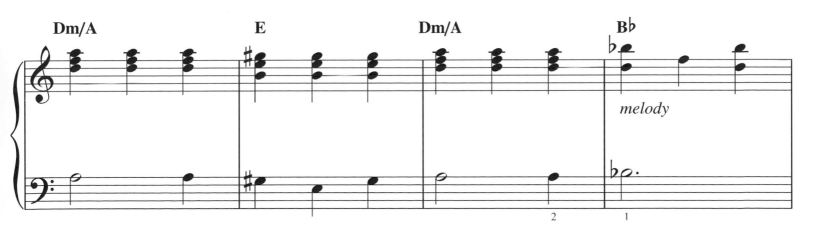

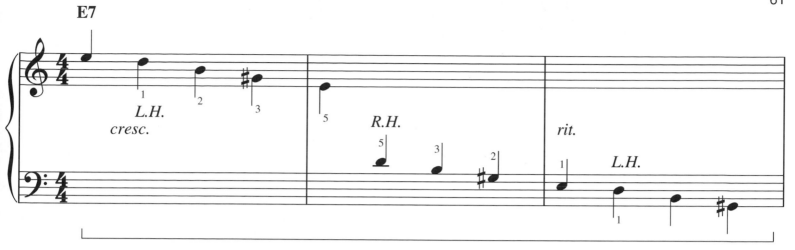

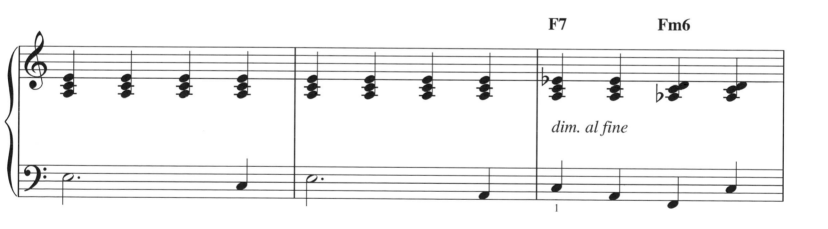

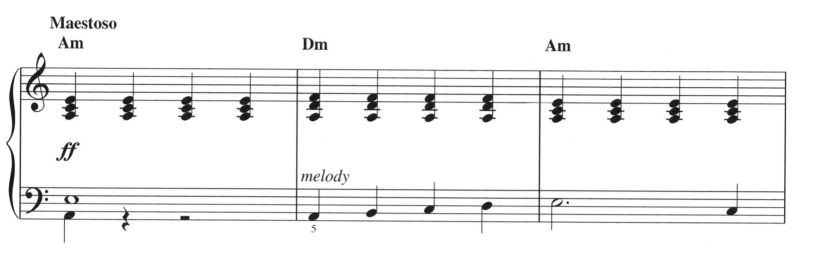

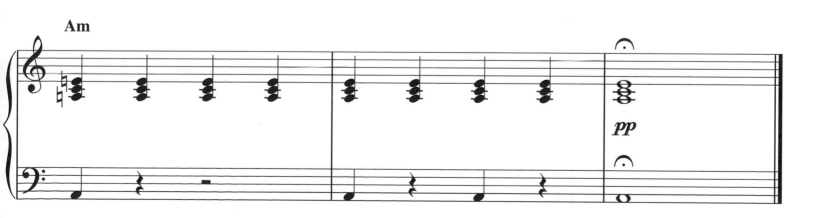

LA DONNA È MOBILE
from RIGOLETTO

By GIUSEPPE VERDI
1813-1901

Allegretto

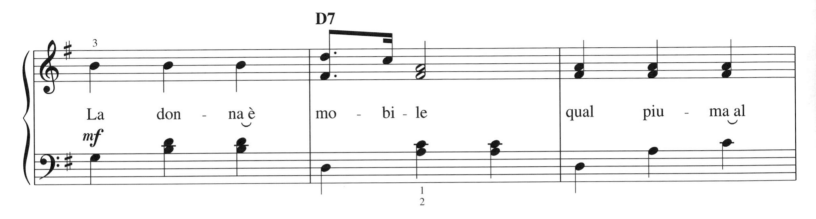

La don - na è mo - bi - le qual piu - ma al

ven - to, mu - ta d'ac - cen - to

e di pen - sie - ro. Sem - pre un a -

ma - bi - le   leg - gia - dro   vi - so,

in   pian - to o in   ri - so,   è   men - zo -

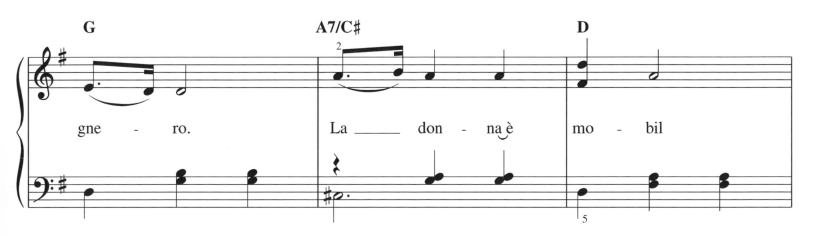

gne - ro.   La ___ don - na è   mo - bil

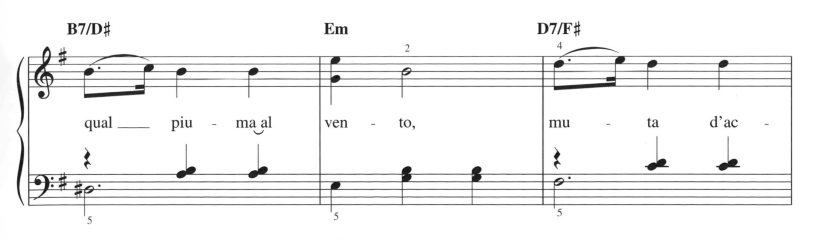

qual ___ piu - ma al   ven - to,   mu - ta   d'ac -

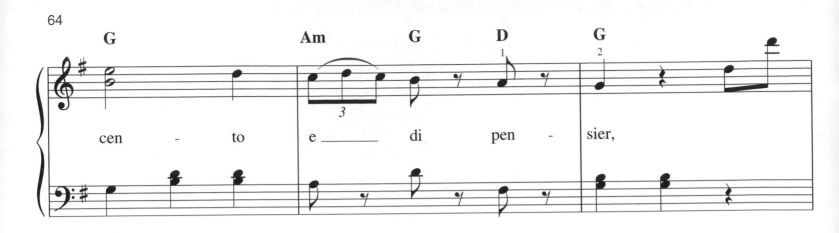

cen - to   e _____ di pen - sier,

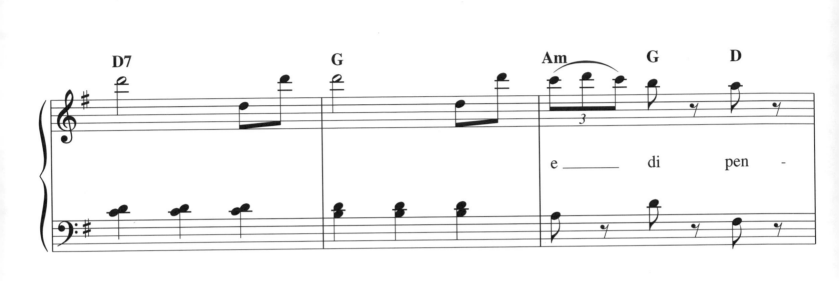

e _____ di   pen -

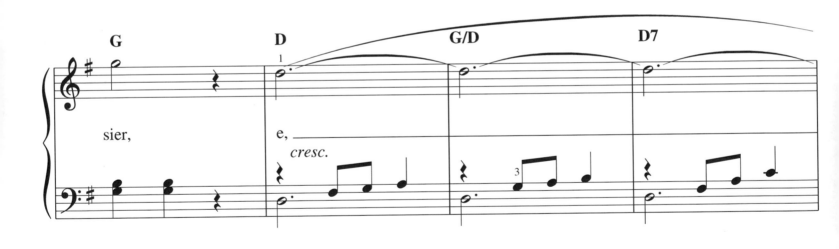

sier,   e, _____
cresc.

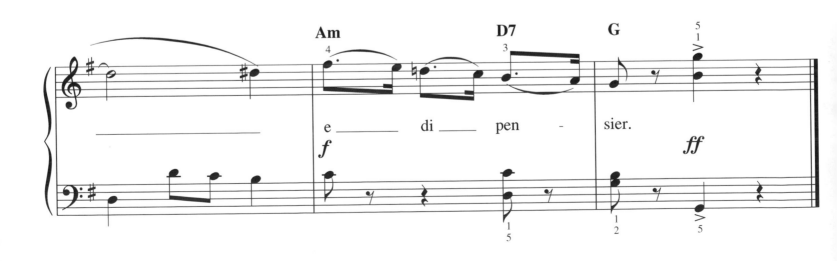

_____   e _____ di _____ pen - sier.
f   *ff*